THE ISLAMIC GOLDEN AGE: SHIPPING AND TRADING LESSONS FROM HISTORY

BY: MUSTAFA NEJEM

CONTENTS

INTRODUCTION

Despite comprising one-fifth of the world's population, Muslims today might not appear to contribute significantly to the global economy and trade practices. However, history tells a different story. Muslims once thrived during a remarkable era of advancements in various aspects of life, from trade and commerce to intellectual discoveries. This period, known as the Islamic Golden Age, unfolded under the rule of Abbasid Caliph Harun al-Rashid and marked a time of great progress and expansion. Notably, establishing the House of Wisdom in Baghdad was pivotal in fostering this era of enlightenment.

This era, spanning from the 8th to the 13th century (although its end is debated, with some citing events like the Mongolian Sack of Baghdad in 1258 or the completion of the Christian Reconquista in 1492), stands as a golden period for Muslims. During this time, they thrived economically, politically, and financially and witnessed flourishing advancements in science and culture. Muslim travellers and explorers from various corners of the world embarked on journeys, facilitating the exchange of intellectual ideas and cultural interactions. The House of Wisdom in Baghdad became a major attraction for scholars and intellectuals from around the globe, including individuals from different religious backgrounds. In addition to Baghdad, cities like Cairo and Córdoba emerged as pivotal centres of intellectual activity, where numerous ancient texts were translated into Arabic and vice versa. Remarkably, these endeavours were often sponsored by governments and wealthy individuals who provided financial support to scholars for their intellectual discoveries.

As mentioned earlier, all the discoveries were made possible due to the Muslim world's pioneering work in discovering and modifying papermaking. This innovation later became one of the largest industries of its time, leading to the flourishing book trade, the establishment of numerous libraries, the initiation of translation movements, and even the development of the human printing press. Furthermore, this era's emphasis on knowledge and its economic implications offers valuable lessons for modern businesses in innovation, intellectual capital, diversity, and global knowledge exchange.

As Muslim explorers like Ibn Battuta and Chinese admiral Zheng He travelled extensively, covering vast distances, Muslim scholars like Al-Fazari and Al-Zarqali dedicated their expertise to enhancing navigational instruments such as the astrolabe and quadrant. These remarkable navigational tools enabled precise determination of latitude and accurate course-plotting, significantly reducing the risk of becoming lost at sea.

With the mastery of navigational tools, Muslims also left their mark on the history of shipbuilding, proving themselves as remarkable shipbuilders through the construction of the Dhow ship. These vessels, characterised by their elegant designs and distinctive lateen sails, played a versatile role in maritime history, serving purposes ranging from exploration to fishing. However, Muslim traders predominantly used them for trading and exploration. The unique design of dhows, featuring narrow hulls and efficient lateen sails, made them exceptional navigators capable of sailing through various water conditions. Arab shipbuilders were the architects of these maritime wonders, connecting cultures through trade networks, and their seaworthiness and cargo capacity was unmatched.

When it comes to trade, Muslim traders described many trade routes, such as the Silk Road and Spice Road. These trade networks facilitated connections between regions like East Africa, China, Europe, and the Indian Ocean, expanding overland and maritime routes. Furthermore, their trade allowed the world to access spices, silk, gems, and glass. During that time, cities like Baghdad, Cairo, and Cordoba became thriving trade hubs. Through these hubs, Muslim traders engaged in trade and learned about new cultures, languages, and discoveries. Additionally, they proved themselves as great diplomats, as evidenced by historical treaties like the Treaty of Hudaybiyyah and the Treaty of Najran, highlighting the importance of diplomatic agreements in maintaining peaceful trade relations and emphasising the value of looking beyond immediate gains for long-term benefits.

In this book, we will explore all these aspects of the life of Muslims during the Islamic Golden Age, teaching modern traders that the contributions of Muslims from that era should not be forgotten. We will delve into the aroma of spices and the gentle breeze of Dhow ships to understand the journeys of Muslim explorers of that time, both in trade and intellectual pursuits.

Chapter 1

PAPER AND BOOK TRADE

Without the proper acknowledgement of the contributions made by Islamic traders to the history of papermaking, the narrative of the Islamic Golden Age remains incomplete. Today, it's nearly impossible to envision our lives without the presence of paper.

Even in this modern era dominated by machines, paper use remains steadfast. Consider the nostalgic scent of old books or the fresh, crisp smell of new ones—no matter how reliant we become on machines, they simply can't replicate the tactile pleasure of turning the pages.

If you're one of those book enthusiasts who can't fathom relying solely on a Kindle, extend your gratitude to Muslim traders for bringing this invaluable treasure to the Western world. While it's true that the Chinese originated the invention we know as paper, it was the Muslim explorers who introduced paper to the West and perfected the techniques required for bookmaking.

Furthermore, the Islamic Golden Age played a significant role in advancing papermaking, bridging the gap between a thriving book trade and the widespread distribution of knowledge. This laid the foundation for centuries of intellectual growth and exchange.

In this chapter, we will embark on a journey through the captivating history of papermaking, shedding light on the profound contributions of the Islamic Golden Age to this transformative global process.

THE ISLAMIC GOLDEN AGE CONTRIBUTION TO PAPERMAKING

Muslims played a pivotal role in advancing the art of papermaking, which, in turn, facilitated the growth of the book trade and the widespread sharing of knowledge. It was through their relentless efforts that the transfer of knowledge became a common occurrence. In this manner, contemporary businesses have realised the importance of investing in education and research and the significance of sharing knowledge. This understanding has led to the development an aspect where book trading and exchanging ideas contribute to the economy's growth.

So, let's explore how Muslims acquired the precious commodity of paper, which China guarded for centuries, and what transformative actions they took with it.

HISTORICAL BACKGROUND OF PAPERMAKING

Before the proper use of paper, various regions worldwide relied on alternatives for writing and storing data. These alternatives included papyrus in Egypt and parchment made from animal skin. Even in ancient civilisations, materials like leaves, silk, and clay tablets were used for writing. An example of this practice can be found in the ancient Indus civilisation, where such materials were employed for recording information.

Undoubtedly, paper significantly simplified the lives of writers and record-keepers. Unlike papyrus, paper offered greater stability, reduced the likelihood of cracking, and was far more convenient to store in compact spaces than clay tablets or parchment scrolls. While it's widely believed that the invention of paper originated in China during the first century, it remained a closely guarded secret until the 8th century.

Before Muslims gained knowledge of papermaking, China primarily reserved its use for the elite in society. Surprisingly, it's believed that paper in China was utilised more for wrapping than writing. The Chinese had various uses for it before it eventually found its way into the hands of Muslims.

Initially, paper's origins can be traced back to the inventive work of Cai Lun, around 105 CE, who used ingredients like mulberry, fishnet, and old rags in its creation. It wasn't until the 3rd century that paper officially began to be used for writing. The Chinese even employed it as toilet paper during the 6th century. The Tang dynasty witnessed paper being utilised for storing fragments of information, and the innovation of paper currency emerged during the Song dynasty.

However, the pivotal moment in the story of paper occurs when the Chinese prisoners give up the secret of papermaking with the Muslim conquerors. Muslims' innovations in papermaking techniques

Following the pivotal Battle of Talas between the Muslims and the Chinese in 751, Muslims obtained the technique of papermaking from Chinese prisoners. However, instead of simply adopting the traditional form of paper, they embarked on a journey of innovation and created their unique technique for papermaking. This innovation would go on to have a profound impact on the world.

The process Muslims used for papermaking had its roots in the Chinese traditional process. However, they introduced a significant change by using linen instead of mulberry bark, which was the Chinese standard. In this process, linen rags were collected, soaked, and boiled in water. Subsequently, paper makers allowed them to ferment, contributing to the evolution of their unique papermaking technique.

After cleaning the linen rags to remove dirt and unnecessary chemicals, they used hammers to beat them into pulp. This process transformed the rags into fibres suitable for papermaking. This innovative method resulted in more stable paper and produced thicker sheets, contributing to the widespread use of this advanced paper.

Initially, Muslims were using paper for artistic purposes. However, over time, it evolved into a thriving industry. Baghdad played a pivotal role as the first hub for establishing the paper industry, and from there, its influence spread to other parts of the world.

Furthermore, the journey of the papermaking industry continued its expansion from Baghdad to regions such as Iraq, Syria, and Palestine. From there, it made its way westward. Under Islamic rule during that period, Spain and Morocco established paper industries around 950. Eventually, Europe adopted this industry and evolved it into a larger and highly profitable business. The spread of papermaking profoundly impacted the transmission of knowledge and the development of civilisation.

LESSON FOR MODERN BUSINESSES: INNOVATION IN MATERIALS AND PROCESSES

The innovations brought by Muslims to the paper industry serve as a guidebook for modern innovators, encouraging them to adopt new techniques and further enhance them for the betterment of society. The lesson from the papermaking of the Islamic Golden Age teaches us the value of learning from history to innovate traditional materials and processes.

Furthermore, it underscores the importance of thinking outside the box instead of adhering strictly to old methods, enabling individuals and businesses to stay ahead of their competition. Similarly, this historical example highlights how modern businesses can appreciate and leverage the arts and learning, just as papermaking evolved into an industry due to Muslims' appreciation and widespread use of calligraphy and art during that era.

THE GROWTH OF BOOK TRADE

Certainly, with the establishment of paper mills in various Muslim countries, especially in Baghdad, the availability of books on a larger scale became a reality. It's crucial to remember that a thirst for knowledge deeply drove the Muslims of the Golden Age. Their upbringing and learning from the Quran encouraged them to seek more knowledge. As a result, they wholeheartedly embraced the use of paper and produced books. They initiated book trading activities, creating extensive libraries—a testament to their dedication to scholarship and education.

However, book trading during that era was motivated not solely by profit but by a genuine desire to spread and acquire knowledge from the rich literary and intellectual treasures of other civilisations, notably the Greeks. It was a testament to the Muslims' commitment to expanding their understanding of the world and advancing their contributions to human knowledge and progress.

Also, one of the greatest achievements of that era was the establishment of the first printing industry, which was based on human craftsmanship rather than machines. Notably, the Quran was among the first books copied using this printing press. In addition to the Quran, both fiction and nonfiction works were also painstakingly copied or printed by human hands, showcasing the dedication of scholars and scribes to preserve and disseminate knowledge during the Islamic Golden Age.

Numerous libraries were established during that era, and many books on various topics, including mathematics and science, were copied. This copying process involved meticulous writing and editing, passing from one skilled hand to another. It mirrors the quality control measures in today's writing, where authors must ensure their books are error-free. The professionals responsible for printing and copying books were known as copyists, a highly esteemed profession of the time.

If you're wondering about the financial support for this massive book copying endeavour, it was partially provided by the government but also sponsored by wealthy individuals who funded translators and copyists for their efforts. This thriving industry preserved knowledge and provided economic support to scholars and intellectuals, a truly impressive feat.

Lesson for Modern Businesses: Recognizing the value of information dissemination

Modern businesses should understand how to maintain a passionate commitment to their cause and value the teachings they receive. As the Muslims of the Golden Age were deeply passionate about copying, it reflects their dedication to preserving knowledge. Businesses thrive when they continually acquire knowledge in their field and have a dedicated research committee. It is evident that profits come when someone adheres to high-value teachings, much like how Muslims stuck to the teachings of the Quran and applied them in their lives to thrive. Businesses have the same chance to do so.

THE SPREAD OF KNOWLEDGE

With the establishment of paper mills and the book industry, the dissemination of knowledge became more accessible. Strong evidence of this can be seen in the establishment of numerous libraries and translation hubs.

During the Islamic Golden Age, libraries in various regions also employed translators who translated ancient texts into Arabic, which became a significant industry. During this translation movement, many antique contexts were translated into Arabic and vice versa. Nestorian Christians played a significant role in advancing Arab Islamic civilisation during the Ummayad and Abbasid periods by translating Greek philosophers' writings first into Syriac and then into Arabic. Between the 4th and 7th centuries, scholarly activities in Syriac and Greek languages were either newly initiated or continued from the Hellenistic era. Many valuable ancient texts might have been lost if not for the translation efforts of Arab scholars, who rendered them into Arabic and Persian and later into Hebrew and Latin. Additionally, Islamic scholars incorporated ideas from China and India, and Arabic philosophical literature contributed to the development of modern European philosophy. Hence, papers and books were the primary means for preserving these valuable translated treasures.

LESSON FOR MODERN BUSINESSES: EMBRACE DIVERSITY AND GLOBAL KNOWLEDGE EXCHANGE

The Muslim practice of translating ancient texts can impart a valuable lesson to modern businesses about embracing diversity and promoting knowledge exchange. They can initiate exchange programs with their international partners to better understand their partners' cultural values and customs, facilitating improved interactions. By doing so, businesses can demonstrate to their clients that they are interested in more than just profit. Modern businesses can extend this approach to clients from diverse cultures and even implement programs to translate languages, fostering closer understanding and communication.

ECONOMIC IMPLICATIONS

During the Islamic Golden Age, Muslims flourished in trade, and the economy was in good condition. Consequently, when books became more widespread, it also brought economic prosperity to scholars and students. The government-funded scholars allowed them to pursue knowledge without financial trouble.

Baghdad was a thriving city, and the House of Wisdom stood as a remarkable testament to knowledge exchange. Regardless of religion, people worldwide came together, bringing knowledge and business opportunities. It was a win-win situation for the Muslims of that era.

LESSON FOR MODERN BUSINESSES: INVESTING IN INTELLECTUAL CAPITAL

Baghdad, with the House of Wisdom and its wealth of scholars and libraries, exemplified the concept of intellectual capital during the Islamic Golden Age. While modern businesses may not create entire cities with such intellectual properties, they can draw lessons from this era's emphasis on knowledge evaluation and dissemination. For instance, a branch or department of a business serving as an intellectual capital hub, offering seminars and workshops to other entrepreneurs and industry stakeholders, can attract valuable customers, business partners, and sponsors while sharing and expanding knowledge within their field.

As concluded, Muslims during the Islamic Golden Age demonstrated a deep appreciation for knowledge and pursued it passionately, contributing to their success in various industries of that time. Unlike the Chinese, who guarded the secret of papermaking, Muslims embraced it for a greater purpose. They established libraries, translated numerous texts, and shared knowledge widely among their Muslim counterparts, effectively treating it as a form of trade. Consequently, the Islamic world invested significant effort in copying literature and spreading knowledge. Official libraries supported copyists through paper, and wealthy individuals supported translators. Literature played a pivotal role during the Golden Age of Islam, underscoring the importance of preserving and sharing knowledge across different cultures.

Chapter 2

NAUTICAL INSTRUMENTS AND NAVIGATION

Picture this: huge oceans stretching as far as the eye can see, stars lighting up the night sky, and the salty breeze in your hair. To navigate such waters successfully, ancient sailors wanted more than just a keen sense of path; they required superior gear and strategies. One of the important reasons for developing superior navigation gear through the Islamic Golden Age turned into the prolific exploration undertaken by Muslim students and explorers.

These intrepid travellers embarked on substantial journeys, covering large distances throughout land and sea. Notable amongst them become Ibn Battuta, whose travels spanned from West Africa to Southeast Asia, and Zheng He, a Chinese admiral who voyaged across the Indian Ocean.

The need for unique navigation equipment became obvious as those explorers ventured into uncharted territories and embarked on long sea voyages. Accurate navigation became crucial for their protection and the success of their missions. As a result, Muslim students like Al-Fazari and Al-Zarqali committed their understanding to refining and popularising navigational units just like the astrolabe and quadrant.

These instruments made it possible to decide latitude and, as it should be, plot courses, lowering the danger of having misplaced or encountering perilous waters. Moreover, lessons from these stories highlight the importance of embracing technological improvements in navigation, a subject that continues to resonate in modern maritime alternate.

So, let's embark on a thrilling journey through time, exploring the charming global nature of nautical contraptions and navigation during the Islamic Golden Age. This chapter will dive into the interesting testimonies of amazing navigational contraptions, i.e., the astrolabe and the quadrant. We'll discover how those resourceful gadgets revolutionised sea travel and continue to encourage us nowadays.

INTRODUCTION TO ADVANCED NAUTICAL INSTRUMENTS

Navigating the treacherous waters of the open sea isn't a small feat. Before the advent of GPS and satellite navigation, mariners relied on celebrities, the sun, and a group of first-rate gear to guide them appropriately to their locations. During the Islamic Golden Age, which spanned from the 8th to the thirteenth centuries, Muslim pupils and polymaths made superb advancements in navigation, giving rise to some of the most creative instruments the world has ever seen.

ASTROLABE: A COSMIC NAVIGATOR

Historical Significance: Navigational Prowess of Al-Fazari

Our journey starts with the astrolabe, a tool that resembles a mystic's amulet but holds the strength of the cosmos. It was during this splendid duration that Muslim students, including the awesome Al-Fazari, subtled and popularised the astrolabe. This reputedly complex device performed a pivotal function in converting records.

APPLICATION: NAVIGATING VIA THE STARS

The astrolabe changed into a true surprise. It enabled sailors to calculate their range by measuring the angle between the horizon and our celestial bodies. Imagine being out at sea, surrounded by nothing but countless waves and a sky full of stars. The astrolabe allowed mariners to decipher their role with uncanny accuracy, making daring voyages throughout uncharted waters greater and, most importantly, more secure.

The quadrant, an angular marvel, becomes used to measure the altitude of celestial bodies, such as the solar or specific stars. Sailors would sight the chosen celestial item through the quadrant's sighting mechanism and notice the attitude it shaped with the horizon. This perspective became instrumental in determining their genuine role on Earth, aiding in plotting their course.

QUADRANT: A HEAVENLY ANGLE-MEASURER

Historical Significance: Al-Zarqali's Nautical Ingenuity

Our subsequent instrument of intrigue is the quadrant, an angular surprise. It was invented by the fantastic Muslim polymath Al-Zarqali. They become used to measure the altitude of celestial bodies, such as the solar or specific stars. Sailors would sight the chosen celestial item through the quadrant's sighting mechanism and notice the attitude it shaped with the horizon. This perspective became instrumental in determining their genuine role on Earth, aiding in plotting their course.

APPLICATION: PLOTTING COURSES WITH PRECISION

In the hands of skilled navigators, the quadrant has become a seafaring cornerstone. By watching the angles fashioned between the horizon and stars, sailors could plot their path with extraordinary precision. This newfound accuracy ensured that ships reached their intended locations extra reliably, averting the perils of being lost at sea.

These gadgets had been invaluable for ancient mariners, allowing them to navigate the open seas more accurately and self-assuredly. They decreased the risks of having misplaced at sea and enabled a hit exploration and trade during the Islamic Golden Age. These classes from history inspire the significance of embracing technological improvements in navigation for modern maritime change.

LESSON: EMBRACE TECHNOLOGICAL ADVANCEMENTS IN NAVIGATION

Now that we've exposed the ancient marvels of the astrolabe and quadrant, it's time to extract valuable lessons from those ancient memories of navigation.

To force this factor home, let's turn to the adventures of Ibn Battuta, a renowned Muslim explorer of the 14th century. Ibn Battuta embarked on great travels across the Islamic world, masking distances that might make even the most pro-modern-day vacationer gasp. Yet, what is most high-quality is how he navigated the substantial Sahara Desert and the open seas.

Ibn Battuta's mystery Well, it wasn't a GPS or satellite TV for PC maps. No, it became the astrolabe and quadrant. These trusty contraptions guided him through deserts and oceans, permitting him to discover uncharted territories with unwavering confidence.

LESSON FOR MODERN TRADERS: NAVIGATE TOWARDS SUCCESS

For present-day buyers, there may be a treasured lesson right here. Embrace and invest in cutting-edge navigation technologies, which include GPS, sonar, and advanced mapping structures. These tools, like the astrolabe and quadrant of vintage, ensure a secure and green maritime change in the contemporary world.

Consider this: modern ships crisscross the globe, transporting items from one nook of the arena to another. In this elaborate dance of world change, precise navigation is the key to fulfilment. GPS systems, for example, provide real-time vicinity statistics, helping ships chart their path as they should and avoid collisions. These current marvels ensure that exchange routes are optimised, transport times are decreased, and the right of entry to markets is increased.

THE IMPACT ON TRADE ROUTES

To respect the importance of embracing technological advancements, let's journey back in time. Imagine a bustling hub of exchange inside the heart of the Indian Ocean, wherein various cultures converge to change goods, thoughts, and know-how.

Enter Zheng He, a Chinese admiral and Muslim dealer whose name is synonymous with grandeur. Zheng He launched a chain of epic voyages during the Ming Dynasty in the early fifteenth century. His treasure fleets sailed a long way and wide, traversing the big expanse of the Indian Ocean. His reliance on advanced navigational tools made those voyages even more excellent.

Zheng He's ships had been ready with the state-of-the-art navigational generation, such as the astrolabe and quadrant. These gears now facilitate change and foster cultural alternates and knowledge switches. The result? Flourishing change routes, in which items, thoughts, and those flowed freely.

LESSON FOR MODERN TRADERS: NAVIGATE TOWARDS PROSPERITY

Modern traders can draw an essential lesson from Zheng He's adventures. Utilise the modern-day navigation era to optimise change routes, reduce shipping times, and expand the marketplace. Just because the astrolabe and quadrant opened up new horizons for historic mariners, present-day navigation gear can release a world of possibilities for ultra-modern investors.

Consider the Suez Canal, a present-day engineering surprise that shortens the maritime course between Europe and Asia. GPS navigation is pivotal in guiding ships accurately through this slim channel, lowering transit instances and costs for infinite organisations.

SAFETY AND EFFICIENCY

Now, let's challenge the area of protection and efficiency, wherein the classes from beyond hold resonate nowadays.

The Islamic Golden Age became a period of enlightenment marked by medical and cultural achievements. One such success was the development of astrolabes and quadrants, significantly decreasing the hazards of shipwrecks and navigational errors.

Picture this: a crew of sailors counting on the celebs and their trusty astrolabes to guide them appropriately home. The accuracy of those devices made the difference between life and death in the course of perilous voyages.

LESSON FOR MODERN TRADERS: PRIORITIZE SAFETY AND EFFICIENCY

For present-day traders, protection and performance are non-negotiable. Embracing present-day navigation gadgets and ensuring that personnel are well-educated about their use is paramount. This investment no longer only mitigates risks but additionally ensures the clean operation of maritime alternate.

Think about the radar systems mounted on ships these days. These superior technologies can locate other vessels, determine limitations, and even convert weather conditions, allowing captains to make informed choices and avoid potential dangers. It's a far cry from the uncertainty faced by mariners of the beyond.

ENVIRONMENTAL CONSIDERATIONS

Our adventure through the annals of history takes us to an area where navigation changed into achieving a destination and respecting the sensitive stability of the herbal international.

In the days of antiques, Muslim traders navigated by way of celebrities and environmental cues, showing a deep appreciation for the arena around them. They understood the importance of harmonising with nature, and this ethos guided their maritime practices.

LESSON FOR MODERN TRADERS: EMBRACE SUSTAINABLE PRACTICES

While we eagerly embrace technological improvements, we must also be mindful of the environmental effects of our actions. Modern traders must undertake sustainable practices in maritime change, not just because it's responsible but also because it's vital for preserving our planet's sensitive ecosystems.

Consider the shift towards purifiers and extra-efficient propulsion systems, which include liquefied natural gas (LNG) and electric engines. These innovations reduce emissions, reduce the ecological footprint of delivery, and pave the way for an extra-sustainable maritime industry.

CONTINUOUS LEARNING

Our voyage through time would not be complete without emphasising the significance of non-stop studying and innovation.

During the Islamic Golden Age, the development and refinement of nautical gadgets resulted from continuous learning and innovation. Scholars and seafarers alike had been committed to pushing the feasible.

LESSON FOR MODERN TRADERS: FOSTER A CULTURE OF INNOVATION

Modern investors ought to heed this undying lesson. Encourage a tradition of continuous study and innovation within your business enterprise. By doing so, you may stay at the forefront of navigation technology and practices, ensuring that your operations are not simply efficient but additionally resilient in the face of unexpected changes on the international front.

Consider the upward push of self-sustaining delivery, in which synthetic intelligence and system study are used to navigate vessels. This groundbreaking generation promises to increase efficiency and decrease the capability for human mistakes, marking the next frontier in maritime exchange.

As we finish this epic adventure through the annals of maritime history, we find ourselves on the cusp of a new generation in navigation. The training we've gleaned from the past is more applicable than ever as cutting-edge buyers navigate the complexities of global trade.

The astrolabe and quadrant, revered as the pinnacle of navigational innovation, have given way to various current marvels: GPS, satellite TV for PC conversation, advanced mapping systems, and sustainable practices. These gears have reshaped the maritime industry, making it safer, more efficient, and more environmentally accountable.

Our voyage through history reminds us that innovation, adaptability, and admiration for the environment are the compass points that guide us towards achievement. By embracing technological advancements, prioritising protection, adopting sustainable practices, and fostering a non-stop lifestyle, gaining knowledge of and innovation, contemporary buyers can chart a course to prosperity in the ever-evolving world of maritime change.

So, fellow adventurers, as you navigate the seas of these days and tomorrow, may you additionally find inspiration in the tales of those who came earlier, and may your journey be marked through secure passage, efficient routes, and a commitment to keeping the beauty of our planet.

In the massive tapestry of history, certain eras shine with a brilliance that transcends time. The Islamic Golden Age changed into one such epoch, wherein mind and tradition flourished in concord. Yet, as we embark on our historic voyage, we'll discover an often unnoticed side of this period: the captivating realm of dhow ships and the long-lasting art in their construction.

The Islamic Golden Age stands as a beacon, a time when scholars illuminated the sector with their awareness and the seas bore witness to the graceful sails of dhows, sporting the flame of civilisation on remote beaches.

In this chapter, we'll discover the timeless awareness and classes that these vessels and their shipbuilding strategies offer to present-day shipbuilders. Join us on this journey as we unveil the fascinating world of dhow ships, delving into their versatility, seaworthiness, and the artistry of Arab shipbuilders.

EXPLORATION OF DHOW SHIPS AND THEIR ADVANTAGES

The Versatile Dhow Ship

Imagine standing on the seashores of ancient Arabia, gazing out on the horizon, where the sun kisses the sea. At that moment, you might have witnessed a majestic dhow gracefully gliding across the water, its distinct lateen sails billowing within the breeze. Dhows, with their stylish designs, have always ignited the imaginations of sailors and history lovers alike, weaving memories of journeys and change in the open waters.

These superb vessels came in an enchanting array of sizes and configurations, each crafted with a selected maritime motive. Whether it changed into the bustling alternate routes that weaved difficult cultural connections, daring voyages of exploration into uncharted territories, or the tranquil art of fishing, dhows left an indelible mark on the pages of history.

But let's rewind the clock, travelling again in time to the coronary heart of historic Arabia. Here, amid the sands and shimmering seas, the understanding of delivery design and production has been meticulously honed over centuries. It's here that the tale of the dhow really begins, with its layout characterised by a narrow hull and people's exclusive triangular sails that were no longer smooth on the eyes but surprisingly useful too. These sails, called lateen sails, would capture the wind gracefully, propelling the dhow ahead with beauty and performance.

OVERVIEW OF DHOW SHIP DESIGN, SIZE, AND STRUCTURE:

The dhow's layout was a surprise to maritime engineering. Its slender, lengthy hull allowed it to go with the flow through the water with minimum resistance, even as its triangular lateen sails captured the wind correctly. Dhows got here in various sizes, from small fishing boats to huge trading vessels, every meticulously crafted to fulfil its supposed purpose.

HISTORICAL ROLES OF DHOWS IN TRADE, EXPLORATION, AND FISHING:

Its versatility was unmatched. It served as an essential hyperlink within the substantial trade networks of the Indian Ocean, connecting cultures and facilitating the exchange of products, thoughts, and technologies. Dhows also played a massive role in exploration, exemplified by the famed navigator Ibn Majid, who guided ships through treacherous waters. Moreover, those vessels were critical for sustenance, permitting communities to thrive via fishing.

SEAWORTHINESS AND EFFICIENCY

The secrets and techniques of dhow design extended far beyond mere aesthetics; they unlocked the treasures of seaworthiness and efficiency. The specific traits of dhows made them masterful navigators, capable of traversing numerous waters with grace and ease. Their shipment-retaining capacities had been equally wonderful, enabling them to ferry goods across vast expanses, setting the stage for thriving exchange networks.

HOW DHOW DESIGN CONTRIBUTED TO THEIR SEAWORTHINESS IN DIVERSE WATERS

The innovative design of the dhows allowed them to navigate a huge variety of water conditions, from calm coastal waters to the tumultuous seas of the Indian Ocean. The aggregate of the lateen sails and a shallow draft made them surprisingly manoeuvrable and properly suitable for lengthy voyages and shallow harbours.

ADVANTAGES OF DHOWS IN NAVIGATION AND CARGO CAPACITY

Dhows had been prised for their potential to carry massive shipments. Their spacious holds allowed for transporting goods, including spices, textiles, and valuable metals, across enormous distances. This efficient use of area made them essential to the bustling exchange routes that linked regions as diverse as the Arabian Peninsula, India, and East Africa.

TRADITIONAL SHIPBUILDING TECHNIQUES

THE CRAFTSMANSHIP OF ARAB SHIPBUILDERS

Under the graceful exterior of every dhow lay the meticulous craftsmanship of Arab shipbuilders. These skilled artisans have been the architects of maritime goals, pouring their knowledge into each inch of their creations. Shipbuilding held a sacred place in the Arab way of life, symbolising a profound connection between humanity and the sea.

THE ROLE OF SKILLED CRAFTSMEN IN DHOW SHIPBUILDING

Arab shipbuilders were respected for their craftsmanship, and the construction of dhows was a labour of love. Skilled craftsmen, often part of specialised shipbuilding communities, meticulously decided on substances, fashioned hulls, and rigged sails to perfection. This attention to detail ensured the seaworthiness and toughness of every vessel.

THE HISTORICAL SIGNIFICANCE OF SHIPBUILDING IN ARAB CULTURE

Shipbuilding has become no longer just a career but a cultural cornerstone for Arab societies. The capacity to craft vessels that could navigate the open seas became a source of pleasure and status. It linked groups and facilitated the change of understanding and traditions.

THE ART OF DHOW SHIPBUILDING

Dhow shipbuilding became more than a mere craft; it became an artwork. Arab shipbuilders harnessed regionally sourced materials and centuries-old construction methods, passing down their understanding through generations. The technique served as a testament to the collaborative spirit of shipbuilding groups, wherein know-how and ability converged to craft maritime masterpieces.

MATERIALS AND CONSTRUCTION TECHNIQUES USED IN DHOW SHIPBUILDING

Arab shipbuilders preferred teak and rosewood for their durability and resistance to the harsh marine environment. These materials had been expertly joined together using conventional strategies, together with mortise-and-tenon joints and timber pegs. The result was a robust, flexible, and seaworthy vessel.

THE COLLABORATIVE NATURE OF SHIPBUILDING COMMUNITIES:

The construction of a dhow became a network effort. Shipbuilders, sailmakers, and riggers laboured collectively, passing on their information from one era to the next. This collaborative technique no longer only ensured the success of every challenge but also fostered an experience of solidarity and shared purpose within the community.

LESSON: ADAPTING TRADITIONAL SHIPBUILDING TECHNIQUES TO MODERN NEEDS

Modernisation of Shipbuilding As we navigate the currents of history, we observe the evolution of shipbuilding technology from the time of dhows to the generation of cutting-edge vessels. The classes derived from traditional delivery design and construction are an undying reminder that innovation often reveals its roots in the past. This is a testament to the long-lasting relevance of the Golden Age's legacy.

The transition from dhows to modern vessels marked a tremendous jump in the shipbuilding era. Innovations, which include iron and metal hulls, diesel engines, and advanced navigation systems, transformed the maritime industry. Yet, the essential ideas of green layout and using local materials remain applicable.

LESSONS LEARNED FROM TRADITIONAL SHIP DESIGN AND CONSTRUCTION

Dhow ships, the graceful marvels of the ocean, have forever captivated the hearts of sailors and history enthusiasts. Imagine their one-of-a-kind lateen sails billowing gracefully in the wind while the vessel glides easily through the water. These dhows had no person-trick ponies; they arrived in a spectacular array of configurations and dimensions, every tailor-made to conquer an exceptional slice of the maritime world.

Picture this: bustling alternate routes that crisscrossed the open seas, connecting cultures, buying and selling goods, and fostering a tapestry of alternate Dhows have been the threads that weave this intricate internet of trade. They have been the bold adventurers of their time, venturing into uncharted waters and paving the way for discoveries yet to come. And, amid it all, they even determined time for the tranquil artwork of fishing, offering sustenance for infinite coastal communities.

But where did these maritime marvels originate? The story takes us back to the cradle of civilisation itself, ancient Arabia. Over the centuries, the delivery design and production craft have been meticulously honed. The dhow, with its slender hull and those iconic triangular sails, changed into more than just a pretty face; it became a masterstroke of each form and feature. So, the next time you gaze upon a dhow, remember that it is now not only a vessel but a piece of dwelling history crafted with skill and destined for a journey at the high seas. B. Incorporating local knowledge and expertise.

EXAMPLES OF REGIONS WHERE TRADITIONAL SHIPBUILDING KNOWLEDGE IS PRESERVED

In numerous corners of the sector, traditional shipbuilding techniques undergo. From the intricacies of Norwegian timber boat production to the craftsmanship of Indonesian shipwrights building Phinisi schooners, those areas preserve a connection to their maritime heritage. The renovation of those strategies serves as a testament to the enduring price of conventional shipbuilding information.

COLLABORATIVE EFFORTS BETWEEN TRADITIONAL AND MODERN SHIPBUILDERS FOR INNOVATION

Forward-questioning shipbuilders recognise the potential of merging traditional wisdom with cutting-edge technology. Collaborations among pro artisans and present-day engineers yield vessels that embrace the first-class of both worlds. These hybrid ships are designed for performance, sustainability, and ancient reverence.

The story of Ibn Majid, the mythical Arab navigator, transports us through uncharted waters, unveiling the richness of his contributions. His information on navigation, cartography, and guiding dhows continues to encourage contemporary sailors and explorers, reminding us of the enduring impact of his legacy. Ibn Majid's navigational prowess was instrumental in facilitating dhows' motion alongside elaborate trade routes. His know-how of the celebrities, currents, and coastal landmarks was nothing short of wonderful, permitting mariners to navigate the widespread expanse of the Indian Ocean with self-assurance. His well-known work, the "Book of the Benefits of the Principles of Navigation," remains a treasure trove of maritime understanding, imparting undying insights into the artwork of navigation.

THE RESURGENCE OF TRADITIONAL DHOWS IN CARGO SHIPPING

In an age marked by the use of gigantic steel behemoths, a sudden revival of interest in traditional dhows for shipment delivery has emerged. These vessels constitute eco-friendly alternatives, embodying the sustainability values of a bygone generation and supplying a fresh attitude towards maritime transportation.

The resurgence of dhows in cargo shipping is a testament to their enduring practicality and environmental friendliness. Dhows rely on wind electricity, reducing their carbon footprint compared to fossil-gasoline-powered vessels. In areas just like the Arabian Gulf and the East African coast, dhows are becoming a preferred choice for transporting goods.

SUSTAINABLE SHIP DESIGN: LESSONS FROM TRADITIONAL BOATBUILDERS

Today's eco-aware global appears to conventional boatbuilders as an idea. Their tried and authentic strategies and substances guide the improvement of sustainable delivery designs intending to shield our oceans and guard our planet for future generations.

INCORPORATING SUSTAINABLE MATERIALS

Traditional shipbuilders often desired sustainable substances like wood, which can be sourced domestically and renewably. Modern shipbuilders are rediscovering the price of wood and other sustainable materials, which reduce the environmental impact of ship construction and operation.

EFFICIENCY AND REDUCED EMISSIONS:

Lessons from conventional ship layout, emphasising green use of space and power, influence the development of eco-friendly vessels. These ships are designed to reduce emissions and gasoline consumption, contributing to a cleaner and more sustainable maritime industry.

In the end, the legacy of dhow ships and traditional shipbuilding techniques from the Islamic Golden Age continues to shine an illuminating light on our path ahead. Their versatility, seaworthiness, and the artistry of Arab shipbuilders remain evergreen sources of inspiration. As we chart our course via the complicated seas of the cutting-edge world, allow us to heed the decision to explore and adapt these time-honoured methods, ensuring that the legacy of innovation and craftsmanship from the Golden Islamic Age endures. In doing so, we honour the beyond and set sail closer to a brighter maritime future, guided by the undying awareness of the dhow ships. The journey of discovery and innovation continues, with the dhow as our timeless compass, guiding us towards a sustainable and harmonious relationship with the ocean.

Chapter 3

TRADING NETWORKS
AND TRADE ROUTES

The development of trade and long-distance relationships during the past several thousand years certainly did shape the course of world history. If there is one thing that is evident from ancient world history, it is that distances were conquered. People, animals, materials, and information moved about without regard for mountains or oceans.

Historians have located evidence of Arab trade networks over more than 1,000 years. Through the development of these networks and their integration into the larger world system, Muslims helped to establish and build civilisations. The Arab world is the birthplace of three monotheistic religions and cultures that have shaped and influenced modern-day society. Expanding on ancient land and sea trade routes, the Muslim traders' legacy continues today through economic endeavours such as NAFTA (North American Free Trade Agreement). Throughout the history of Arab influence in world culture, the Arab peoples have controlled many trade networks. The Sassanid and Abbasid Empires were just some of the apexes of the massive Arab powers. The Arabs established trade routes from East Africa to China and Europe to the Indian Ocean.

The Golden Islamic Age is when Islam impacted many parts of the world, including Northern Africa, Spain, Andalusia, and Central Asia. It is attributed to trade routes during this era that connected these lands that were once cut off. Through these trade places, spices, silk, gems, and glass became much more accessible globally. Many of us are familiar with the legendary caravans that counted a community of traders from China, India, and Egypt. To uncover this well-kept mystery, we'll have to go back to talk about the Golden Islamic Age!

EXTENSIVE ARAB TRADE NETWORKS

The Arabs' extensive trade networks are a testament to their ability to adapt and trade with the world. This trade was facilitated by an extensive network of roads and sea routes that connected the different regions within the Arab Empire. They also had a very flexible system of weights and measures and a unique monetary system that included paper money called "girsh" or "dirham."

These factors enabled them to deal with people worldwide without having trouble understanding each other's systems or agreeing on how much something was worth in terms of currency or weight.

THE ARABIAN PENINSULA: ORIGINS OF ARAB TRADE

The earliest known civilisation in Arabia was centred around the oasis of Teima (now part of modern-day Saudi Arabia). The people who lived there were called Nabataeans; they were nomadic herders who had mastered irrigation systems for water and agriculture. They built many cities throughout their territory, including Petra (which means "rock" in Greek), where they carved elaborate buildings into the stone cliffs that surrounded it.

The Nabataeans traded with other civilisations all over the Mediterranean Sea through land routes across Arabia and the Red Sea coast. They traded spices like cinnamon, frankincense, myrrh, and cumin for glassware from Egypt, as well as fabrics from Persia. They also exported metals like lead, iron ore, copper ore, silver ore, gold ore—and even tin (often mixed with copper).

EARLY TRADE PRACTICES IN THE ARABIAN PENINSULA

The earliest recorded trade practices in this area date back to around 2400 BCE, when sea-faring merchants began trading goods between Egypt and Mesopotamia (modern-day Iraq). Over time, this expanded into a huge network of traders who moved goods from place to place along what became known as the Incense Route. The Incense Route was one of the most critical trade routes throughout history because it connected Europe with China through Egypt and India.

Trade continued throughout most of history when Western powers began taking control of these routes and stopped allowing other merchants access to them.

ROLE OF CAMEL CARAVANS IN DESERT TRADE

To begin with, it was camels that allowed this trade to flourish. The camel caravans used in early Arab trade could travel through the desert at a steady pace, carrying goods between towns and villages. It allowed for even greater distances between towns and villages to be travelled by caravans than if they had been travelling on foot.

The caravans were often led by a merchant or trader who would travel with his family or a small group of assistants along with several hundred camels carrying goods such as spices (including pepper), incense, and precious metals (like gold). The merchants usually used wells to water their camels before heading out again on another leg of their journey.

THE SILK ROAD CONNECTION: LINKING EAST AND WEST

The Islamic Golden Age was a time of great prosperity and cultural exchange. By the 9th century, Arab merchants travelled across the Middle East, Central Asia, and China to trade goods like silk, woollen textiles, spices, precious metals, and jewels. This trade route was known as the Silk Road. Trading networks linked people from all over the world who shared similar interests.

The Silk Road had three main branches:

- The northern branch ran through Central Asia along the steppes of Mongolia

- The central one ran through Persia (modern-day Iran) and Afghanistan

- The southern route went through India and Southeast Asia

These branches linked together at important trading centres like Samarkand and Bukhara (modern-day Uzbekistan).

THE SILK ROAD'S PIVOTAL ROLE IN GLOBAL TRADE

The Silk Road, a network of trade routes connecting East and West, is one of the most critical factors in global trade today. It was a major source of cultural exchange between the two continents and allowed for the movement of goods and people across vast distances.

The Silk Road was originally established by the Han Dynasty (130 BCE-1453 CE) as an overland route from China to Central Asia, India, and Persia. The Silk Road connected China with Europe through Central Asia, India, Persia, and Arabia. It also helped connect Europe with Africa through Egypt and Ethiopia.

ARAB TRADERS' CONTRIBUTIONS TO SILK ROAD COMMERCE

The Silk Road connects China with the West, but it also connects all of Asia. The Arab traders' contributions to Silk Road commerce are just as important as any other group. The Arabs had their version of a "Silk Road" that connected ports on the Red Sea with cities in China and India.

In addition to being an early adopter of the Silk Road trade routes, Arab traders contributed significantly towards opening up China's borders to foreigners by bringing them into contact with people from other cultures through trade agreements.

MARITIME TRADE: NAVIGATING THE SEAS

The golden age of Islamic trade is often remembered as a time of peace and prosperity, but the reality is that these traders were navigating treacherous waters.

The first challenge to overcome was the problem of finding their way across the open sea. The Arabian peninsula had long been a source of conflict for the region's various civilisations, with warring factions cutting off trade routes.

To navigate these seas, traders had to rely on traditional cartographic methods such as celestial navigation and dead reckoning. Celestial navigation involved using the sun and stars to determine one's position at sea, while dead reckoning relied on keeping track of distance travelled based on speed and direction information from navigators aboard ship.

While this may seem rudimentary compared to today's satellite-based GPS technology, it was remarkably effective. It worked well enough that Arab merchants could reach China before Europeans did so themselves!

ARAB SEAFARERS AND THEIR IMPACT ON THE INDIAN OCEAN TRADE

The Indian Ocean has been one of the world's most important bodies of water for centuries. It's home to some of the most important trading routes in history and has been host to various cultures and civilisations.

Arab seafarers were a driving force in the Indian Ocean trade. They were able to navigate across oceans and trade goods throughout the region. Because of this, they greatly impacted the economy of countries located near the sea.

In addition to their cultural contributions, the Arabs also played an important role in improving navigation techniques for ocean voyages around Africa and Asia during this time (collectively known as the Age of Discovery). It included improvements like better charts or maps that would help sailors navigate safely at sea, better ships with larger holds to carry more cargo, better compasses to tell which direction they were going while sailing, etcetera!

The Arabs also greatly impacted Indian Ocean trade because they brought many new ideas and technologies from other countries into India and China, which helped them develop more advanced civilisations than before."

1.   ECONOMIC IMPACT

Arab traders were responsible for bringing Indian spices and cloth to Europe, and they also introduced new technological innovations like the compass and astrolabe.

2.   POLITICAL IMPACT

Arab traders also played an important political role in the region, acting as middlemen between East and West. They helped to facilitate trade between countries like China and India on one side and Europe on the other.

3.   CULTURAL EXCHANGE IMPACT

The influx of Arab traders into the Indian Ocean also had strong cultural impacts; they brought many new ideas about religion, science, and society that would radically change how people thought about their lives.

4.   TECHNOLOGICAL IMPACT

Finally, Arab seafarers also had a significant technological impact on the region through their use of new navigational tools such as compasses and astrolabes, which made it much easier for them to travel long distances across open oceans without getting lost or running out of food supplies during long voyages across vast stretches of open water.

Ports and trading posts along maritime routes

The most important port in Arabia was Jeddah, located on a peninsula at the Red Sea. The port was a hub for trading with India, Africa, and China. From Jeddah, ships could travel to Mecca, Medina, and other nearby cities. Other ports along the Red Sea included Aden in Yemen and

Mogadishu in Somalia. East Africa had two important ports: Mogadishu in Somalia and Zanzibar in Tanzania. These two ports were connected by trade routes through Ethiopia's highlands. In Southeast Asia, several ports were used by Arabs for trading purposes: Malacca (Malaysia), Brunei (Brunei), and Aceh (Indonesia).

LESSONS FROM THE GOLDEN ISLAMIC AGE

Trade networks are the most critical aspect of any economy, and they have been since the dawn of civilisation. Trade was the primary driver of growth and prosperity in the Golden Islamic Age. The Muslim world enjoyed a period of unprecedented expansion during that time, partly because they could develop and maintain strong trading partnerships with other countries.

LESSON 1: FOSTER AND EXPAND TRADE NETWORKS

The Golden Islamic Age was an era of unprecedented economic prosperity. During this time, Muslims established trade networks worldwide and built an empire from Spain to China. The wealth gained from these trade routes helped support their military conquests, which expanded their Empire even further.

CASE STUDY: THE SILK ROAD'S LEGACY IN MODERN CHINA'S BELT AND ROAD INITIATIVE

The Silk Road was an ancient network of trade routes that connected the East and West, including China, India, the Middle East, and Europe. It flourished from the 2nd century BCE to the 15th century CE.

The Silk Road's trade network legacy remains in modern China's Belt and Road Initiative (BRI). The BRI is a multibillion-dollar infrastructure and investment program that aims to connect Asia with Europe via trade routes across Eurasia.

China's BRI covers approximately 65 countries, including overland transport corridors and maritime networks. The program includes projects like railways, ports, airports, energy pipelines, and communications infrastructure.

Strategies for enhancing trade networks in the 21st century

In the 21st century, fostering and expanding trade networks is important. It can be done through the following strategies:

- Increasing Interdependence through Foreign Direct Investment (FDI)

- Reducing Trade Barriers and Other Obstacles to Trade

- Promoting Multilateralism and Trade Liberalization

LESSON 2: TAP INTO NEW MARKETS

The world is changing, and so are how businesses need to operate. Companies have relied on a single market for their products and services for centuries. But with globalisation and new technology, businesses are becoming more important than ever to expand beyond their home country.

Modern examples of companies expanding into emerging markets

One example of this aspect is Apple. Apple has traditionally been a US-based company, but in recent years, they've started to branch out into other territories with their products—and it's working!

Another great example is Coca-Cola. The beverage giant began as a small business in Georgia before expanding into other areas worldwide. Today, it operates in over 200 countries around the globe!

The role of technology in reaching new customer bases

To reach new markets and grow your business globally, it's not enough to think outside of your country's borders—you also need to utilise modern technology like eCommerce platforms (such as Shopify). These platforms can help you set up websites where customers can purchase goods from anywhere!

LESSON 3: ESTABLISH CROSS-REGIONAL TRADE ROUTES

Cross-regional trade routes were established during the Islamic Golden Age to connect the regions and facilitate trade.

The significance of cross-regional connectivity for economic growth

The significance of cross-regional connectivity for economic growth is evident in the history of the Islamic Golden Age. The Islamic world was highly physically and economically interconnected, allowing for trade routes that spanned large distances. This interconnectedness increased demand and the ability to produce goods at scale.

Building infrastructure and logistics for efficient cross-regional trade

To build infrastructure that supports efficient cross-regional trade, it is vital first to understand how a region's geography affects its ability to trade with other regions. For example, high mountain ranges and deserts can disrupt trade routes by making them difficult or impossible to traverse without special equipment or knowledge of the terrain.

REAL-LIFE EXAMPLES AND ANECDOTES

Islamic Golden Age was a time of immense growth and prosperity, with Muslims at the forefront of exploration, astronomy, mathematics, and philosophy. The Islamic world began to flourish during this period.

A. IBN BATTUTA: THE GLOBE-TROTTING EXPLORER AND MERCHANT

One of the most famous examples of the Islamic Golden Age is Ibn Battuta, born in Tangier in 1304. He became a globe-trotting explorer and merchant. He set out on a journey at age 21 through the Islamic world. He travelled to Asia, Africa, and Europe, making it as far as China and India before returning home after 24 years. During his travels, he visited many places in China, Turkey, Russia, and Africa. He also wrote about his experiences in his autobiography titled Rihla (meaning 'travel' 'journey').

B. THE HOUSE OF WISDOM: A CENTRE OF KNOWLEDGE AND TRADE IN BAGHDAD

The House of Wisdom was a centre of learning and trade in Baghdad, founded by Caliph al-Mamun. It was one of the first libraries in the world and remained open until 1258. The library was known for its wide collection of books on all subjects, including astronomy, medicine, mathematics, law, geography, and history. The library also contained works from Christian scholars, allowing scholars from both religions to study together.

C. IBN KHALDUN: THE ECONOMIST AND HISTORIAN'S INSIGHTS ON TRADE AND SOCIETY

Ibn Khaldun was a 14th-century Muslim scholar and historian widely considered one of the most important thinkers in Islamic history. He was born in Tunis and studied at the University of Damascus before becoming a judge in Seville and then moving to Granada, where he served as a finance minister.

Ibn Khaldun wrote many books on economics and history, but his most famous work is Muqaddimah (An Introduction to History), translated into multiple languages. In it, he outlined his theories on human society, including the idea that civilisations rise and fall through cycles of growth, prosperity, decline, and decay. This theory became known as "the Khaldunian cycle.

Overall, drawing from centuries of trade and entrepreneurship, Arab merchant networks left an indelible mark on the world as we know it. By evoking the spirit and lessons of Arab trade, today's globalised world can draw upon these historical trading networks' talent, ingenuity, and resourcefulness to lay a lasting foundation for tomorrow's global economy.

Chapter 4

TRADE CENTRES AND MARKETPLACES

Trade centres are more than just marketplaces; they are cultural capitals that contribute significantly to a country's identity. During the Islamic Golden Age, there were several renowned trade centres, such as Baghdad, Cairo, and Cordoba. These cities facilitated trade and the exchange of goods and became hubs for exchanging knowledge and culture. Merchants worldwide flocked to these centres, bringing their products and the wisdom of their lands. In return, these trade centres enriched the Islamic world with diverse ideas and treasures of knowledge.

The prosperity of trade centres is not limited to business alone; it extends to the overall advancement of civilisation. Trade centres stimulate economic growth by fostering commerce, bringing goods, and generating wealth. Additionally, they promote cultural exchange, leading to a more vibrant and interconnected world.

In this chapter, we delve into the significance of those historical change facilities and draw classes for current corporations on the way to expand change hubs, create attractive marketplaces, and facilitate the trade of products, services, and thoughts to boost economic growth.

THE HISTORICAL PERSPECTIVE

Baghdad: The House of Wisdom and Intellectual Capital

In the coronary heart of the Islamic Golden Age, Baghdad stood as a symbol of information and highbrow capital. The House of Wisdom, a chief highbrow middle in Baghdad, became home to scholars, scientists, and philosophers from diverse backgrounds. It became a melting pot of thoughts, translating and keeping information from various civilisations.

ANECDOTE: THE HOUSE OF WISDOM AS A KNOWLEDGE HUB

The House of Wisdom housed scholars who diligently translated historical texts from Greek, Persian, Indian, and other languages into Arabic. They extended the realm of understanding in arithmetic, astronomy, remedy, and philosophy. This highbrow change laid the muse for amazing improvements.

LESSON: EMBRACE INTELLECTUAL CAPITAL FOR BUSINESS GROWTH.

Modern businesses can learn from Baghdad's embodiment of highbrow capital. Investing in research, improvement, and collaboration can lead to innovation and business growth. Encouraging an environment in which thoughts go with the flow freely and various perspectives are valued can foster creativity and excellence.

CAIRO: THE SILK ROAD AND CULTURAL EXCHANGE

Cairo, situated alongside the Silk Road, played a pivotal role in exchanging products and ideas. This historical change in direction related the East to the West, facilitating the movement of goods, ways of life, and understanding. Cairo became a bustling market in which traders from various lands converged.

The Silk Road brought silk, spices, precious metals, and distinctive goods to Cairo. Along with these products come diverse cultures, languages, and traditions. The town has become a vibrant mosaic of different ethnicities and backgrounds, growing a wealthy and diverse consumer base.

LESSON: PROMOTE CULTURAL EXCHANGE FOR A DIVERSE CUSTOMER BASE

Modern groups can benefit from embracing cultural change. In a globalised world, know-how and respect for extraordinary cultures can entice a broader patron base. Tailoring products and services to the options and customs of numerous communities can result in increased customer loyalty and business fulfilment.

CORDOBA: THE MULTICULTURAL MARKETPLACE

Cordoba, in Islamic Spain, became renowned for its multiculturalism. It was a town where Muslim, Jewish, and Christian groups coexisted and contributed to a flourishing economy. This range extended to the marketplace, making Cordoba a thriving centre of change and trade.

Cordoba became home to scholars, poets, and artists from one-of-a-kind spiritual and cultural backgrounds. It became a town where ideas mingled freely, leading to improvements in fields inclusive of philosophy, technology, and structure. This cultural richness extended to the market, where goods from various regions were sold and offered.

LESSON: CREATE INCLUSIVE MARKETPLACES FOR A THRIVING ECONOMY

Modern companies can learn from Cordoba's inclusivity. Fostering an inclusive marketplace where diverse voices and competencies are welcomed can result in innovation and financial prosperity. Embracing variety within the place of work and in the products or services provided can force enterprise success in a state-of-the-art, interconnected global economy.

INFRASTRUCTURE AND TECHNOLOGICAL ADVANCEMENTS

Investing in modern infrastructure is important for developing exchange hubs. Efficient transportation, communication, and logistics systems are important for the smooth drift of products and services.

LESSON: INVEST IN MODERN TRADE INFRASTRUCTURE FOR EFFICIENCY.

Modern companies need to prioritise infrastructure development. Building contemporary transportation hubs, embracing digital technology for supply chain control, and ensuring efficient logistics can streamline operations and decrease charges.

STRATEGIES FOR DESIGNING APPEALING MARKET SPACES

Designing appealing marketplaces is fundamental to attracting customers. Factors, which include aesthetics, accessibility, and comfort, play essential roles in creating inviting surroundings for shoppers.

LESSON: FOSTER AN INVITING ENVIRONMENT FOR CUSTOMERS

Businesses should be aware of creating attractive and consumer-friendly areas. From the layout and layout of physical stores to consumer-pleasant online platforms, ensuring a wonderful patron experience can result in elevated sales and purchaser loyalty.

EMBRACING GLOBALISATION AND KNOWLEDGE SHARING

In the latest interconnected international context, globalisation and understanding sharing are paramount. Businesses should actively interact with global alternatives and change to stay competitive and progressive.

LESSON: PROMOTE EXCHANGE TO DRIVE ECONOMIC GROWTH

Modern organisations must actively search for possibilities for global exchange and know-how trade. Collaborating with international companions, collaborating in industry activities, and staying knowledgeable about global trends can power monetary growth and competitiveness.

CASE STUDIES

Successful Modern Trade Hubs and Their Impact

Examining case studies of successful cutting-edge change hubs can offer valuable insights for groups. By learning from actual-world examples, businesses can adapt and thrive in an ever-changing international marketplace.

Analysing the studies of current exchange hubs, such as major worldwide airports, delivery ports, and virtual marketplaces, can offer sensible instructions for corporations. These case studies can encourage revolutionary techniques and processes in trade.

The historic change facilities in Baghdad, Cairo, and Cordoba taught us treasured instructions. They emphasised the significance of intellectual capital, cultural change, and inclusivity in fostering thriving economies. These trainings are as relevant nowadays as they were in the past.

ENCOURAGEMENT FOR MODERN BUSINESSES

In the end, current agencies can benefit from those instructions from the Islamic Golden Age. By investing in <u>highbrow capital</u>, promoting cultural alternatives, and embracing inclusivity, agencies can become dynamic trade hubs, create attractive marketplaces, and facilitate the change of products, offerings, and thoughts. In doing so, they could drive monetary growth and success within the global market. Just as the ancient change centres left a long-lasting legacy, modern corporations can leave their mark on the world of trade and innovation.

By embracing these undying instructions, contemporary groups can embark on an adventure towards the handiest monetary boom, cultural enrichment, and worldwide connectivity. They have the energy to shape the destiny of exchange facilities and marketplaces, leaving a legacy that resonates far beyond the goods and offerings they offer—just like Baghdad, Cairo, and Cordoba did in their time.

Chapter 5

INTELLECTUAL PROPERTY PROTECTION

The Islamic Golden Age was filled with remarkable advancements in various fields. It included science, mathematics, medicine, and philosophy. Intellectuals like Ibn Sina (Avicenna) and Al-Razi (Rhazes) contributed significantly to these disciplines. Intellectual property rights, in the form of copyrights and patents, helped protect the works and innovations of these scholars. This protection encouraged them to share their knowledge, knowing their ideas would be safeguarded.

The protection of intellectual property stimulated trade and innovation. Rights to intellectual property also contributed to the dissemination of knowledge. Literature and manuscripts were regarded as precious possessions, and copyright regulations ensured they could be shared, translated, and made available internationally. It helped in facilitating cross-cultural exchanges and trade routes. The environment of IP production and innovation laid the foundation of advancement that was influenced later in Europe. It also contributed to the exchange of knowledge through various trade routes.

In today's globalised economy, protecting intellectual property is very important. This is important because this intellectual property incentivises individuals and other organisations to invest in new technology and brands. This helps in fostering innovation and creativity. It also leads to economic growth. IP protection encourages foreign investment and trade as well. It also ensures fair competition, preventing the unauthorised copying or imitating of goods. Copyright and trademark protection help preserve cultural heritage. It can be done by safeguarding the literature, craftsmanship, and traditional art.

It enables different artists and artisans to continue the tradition and pass to the next generations. The IP protection is also very essential in the international trade. This is because there are different trade agreements, like trade-related aspects of intellectual property rights(TRIPS). This agreement comes under the World Trade Organisation. It set different IP protection standards, which helped promote the harmonisation economy and reduce trade barriers. So, intellectual property is very important in shipping history from the Islamic golden age to the modern world.

RECOGNITION OF THE VALUE OF INTELLECTUAL PROPERTY

The recognition of the value of intellectual property has been evolving. It reflects the changing nature of knowledge and innovation. The Islamic golden age was known for the contributions of numerous intellectual Giants. These include Al Razi, Al Kindi, Al Khuariwzmi, and Al Farabi.

Al Razi made one important contribution. He was a pioneer chemist, physician, and philosopher. He has made significant contributions in the fields of medicine and chemistry. Al Razi wrote a book known as Kitab ul Havi. It was a very influential medical encyclopaedia that influenced many people early in the Islamic golden age. Al Razi has shown his many contributions to the protection of intellectual property.

Islamic scholars highly valued the correct attribution and citation of sources. When his writings were quoted or referred to by other academics, Al-Razi's name and contributions were given due credit, preserving his intellectual presence.

Scholars like Al-Razi frequently enjoyed the backing and patronage of organisations or people who valued their work. This assistance offered resources and safety so that he could keep doing research and writing.

Another intellectual giant was Al Khuariwzmi. He was a Persian astronomer, scholar, and mathematician. He made many contributions to mathematics during the Islamic golden age from the 8th to the 13th century. He has made many contributions to the field of mathematics. His work had a lasting impact on the people who want to learn mathematical concepts. Al Khuariwzmi is also known as the father of algebra. He has published his work known as Al Kitab Al Mukhtasar. This book explains different methods of solving quadratic and linear equations.

Al Khuariwzmi's work was copied by other people as well. So, there was a need for his ownership protection. The Islamic Golden Age was marked by a strong network of scholars and centres of learning. Al-Khwarizmi's work would have been disseminated and protected through this network of scholars, who shared knowledge and ensured its preservation. This helped ensure Al-Khwarizmi received recognition for his contributions when other scholars referenced or cited his works.

ECONOMIC SIGNIFICANCE OF INTELLECTUAL PROPERTY

In the early ages, many historical examples of intellectual property drove trade and prosperity. The Silk Road and the Chinese silk production are one of the most prominent examples. These were the silk production techniques and the silk industry's development for intellectual property protection. The silk trade from the Silk Road helped economic prosperity in China. It also promoted the cultural exchange between the East and West regions.

The adoption of logos, Insignia, and geographic markers contributed to the development of brand identification for goods coming from certain locales or guilds. This branding increased the product's economic value and encouraged trade.

Trade in knowledge-based items was facilitated by intellectual property safeguards, mainly for books and inventions. This encouraged commercial ties between various locations by facilitating the interchange of literature, scholarly manuscripts, and cutting-edge goods through extensive trade channels.

The intellectual property holds a very economic significance in the today's world as well. IP assets can easily be monetised through partnership sales or licensing. It helps the creators and other businesses generate revenue, contributing to financial sustainability. Intellectual property also contributes to the overall economic growth. It is done by fostering innovation, which helps drive productivity, competitiveness, and improvement in the global marketplace. IP rights are also very important for international trade.

The different products and services are protected by intellectual property, which can be exported to the global market. Different trade agreements are done, which set the standards for intellectual property protection. This helps in facilitating cross-border commerce.

HISTORICAL INTELLECTUAL PROPERTY LAWS IN THE ISLAMIC GOLDEN AGE

The protection of manuscripts and scientific writings was important in the Golden Age and other historical periods. Intellectual property protection did not exist, but they had a different copyright-like measure that safeguarded knowledge. Different authors and scholars were credited for their work. It emphasised the importance of recognising the contributions of specific individuals. The copying of the manuscript was allowed, but it was ensured that the copies should have complete accuracy concerning the original text. The manuscripts were considered very valuable possessions. So, these manuscripts include the ownership inscriptions.

In the early times, libraries and Muslim scholars had a great role in preserving knowledge. The libraries were known as the main centres for knowledge. The most common example is the House of Wisdom in Baghdad. In the Islamic golden age, the House of Wisdom was the central place where knowledge was shared and preserved. There was a complete collection of manuscripts that displayed the intellectual heritage.

The Muslim Scholars often write many annotations and commentaries on the existing works. They add their insights into those valuable works, leading to understanding the original text. So, these libraries and Muslim Scholars have facilitated much in transmitting knowledge from one generation to another. So, these libraries and Muslim scholars have facilitated much in transmitting knowledge from generation to generation. It ensured that valuable discoveries were not lost and preserved for a long time. The cities of Timbuktu, Cordoba, and Baghdad were renowned centres for national purposes, the exchange of ideas, and the preservation of knowledge.

LESSONS FOR THE MODERN WORLD

Established Legal Framework for Intellectual Property Protection:

During the Islamic Golden Age, Muslims established a legal framework for intellectual property protection that was remarkably advanced. This framework set the stage for the preservation of knowledge and invention and helped the fields of science, the arts, and commerce to flourish.

The concept of copyright, known as "hifz al-mal" or "protection of property," was introduced. This concept helped recognise the ownership of written works and inventions. Inventions and innovations were also protected. Inventors were given specific rights over their inventions for a specified amount of time, and given that they would have a brief monopoly on their innovations, this incentivised innovators to pass on their discoveries.

Islamic legal scholars and rulers recognised that protecting intellectual property encouraged innovation and knowledge dissemination. This led to the proliferation of libraries, translation centres, and places of learning where intellectual property was valued and respected.

The legal framework ensures that the investors receive rewards for their efforts. The intellectual property laws help in fostering the investment. Companies are more willing to invest in trending technology and products. So, the intellectual property will be protected when they invest in real investors.

It also encourages knowledge sharing through different mechanisms, including technology transfer or licensing for modern businesses. This way, the companies can easily collaborate with the investors, which may lead to different societal advancements and benefits. It can also lead to economic growth, job opportunities, and trade. So, establishing legal frameworks for intellectual property protection is very important in modern societies. This is because they play a very important role in incentivising investment and innovations, which leads to economic growth.

SAFEGUARD INTELLECTUAL PROPERTY RIGHTS:

There was an Ijaza system, which was a formal certification procedure. Ijazas, which served as credentials and licences, were given to academics and artisans. These documents aided in proving the legitimacy and possession of creative works and craft abilities.

Individuals going into internships or partnerships would agree to confidentiality and non-disclosure contracts to protect private knowledge in industries like alchemy, where information was closely monitored.

Craftsmen and artisans frequently formed guilds with rules of behaviour and trade secrets. These guilds assisted in regulating the application of specific techniques and safeguarded the financial interests of those who belonged to them.

One of the primary strategies for modern businesses is taking legal action against the infringers. It involves filing the cases seeking the injunctions and demanding damages in the court. Effective legal representation is crucial for navigating intellectual property litigation by resisting patent trademarks and copyrights with the relevant government authorities. It helps provide you with a strong legal foundation by employing different technologies and surveillance methods for monitoring intellectual property violations.

It involves online monitoring websites, platforms, and supply chains for copyright infringement or counterfeit products. One of the main strategies is also collaborating with the customer authorities. It can be done to intercept the infringing goods and international borders.

There is a great role played by international treaties—one of the vital roles played by the TRIPS agreement. The TRIPS agreement is an international treaty that provides minimum standards for intellectual property protection. It obliged that member countries in this agreement implement different intellectual property protection measures, including trademarks, patents, and copyrights. This agreement also provides different mechanisms for dispute resolution between the member countries and their agreement. It also recognises the importance of helping developing countries build the current property laws.

ENCOURAGING INNOVATION AND SHARING OF IDEAS

The House of Wisdom was known as the hub of innovation and knowledge. The intellectual property was highly protected within the House of Wisdom. It was a centre of innovation and learning. The sharing of knowledge played a pivotal role in the cultural exchange as well as the trade exchange during the golden age. Through the house of wisdom, much new knowledge on different disciplines was shared among the people of different areas in the past, encouraging innovation and technology.

REAL-LIFE EXAMPLES AND ANECDOTES

Al Razi was a Persian scholar. He made many contributions to medicine in the golden age of the 13th century. There were many European Scholars who translated the medical works of Al Razi into the Latin language. This helped a big audience from diverse reasons to understand those medical manuscripts. His manuscript also highlights the importance of intellectual property concerns and the importance of the ownership of the authors in the past.

Another example from the golden age was the impact of Al Khuariwzmi algebra on modern finance in the 8th century. Al Khuariwzmi was a Persian mathematician who developed the principles of algebra. His work has provided great insight into mathematical finance. The Black Scholar Martin model is one of finance's most common algebra examples. This model worked on algebraic equations for calculating the optional prices. He has made many contributions in the algebraic field, which influences financial mathematics and has a big impact on the mathematical innovations in modern finance.

All the above examples illustrate the contemporary and historical relevance of Intellectual Property in various fields.

Overall, intellectual property was significant for knowledge preservation and dissemination during the Islamic Golden Age and in today's world. Similarly, the protection of IP was recognised by patrons, manuscripts and copyright culture. Therefore, all the legal works of Muslim scholars and artists were highly protected using different strategies from being copied without any permission.

Chapter **6**

ROLE OF MUSLIM TRADERS AS CULTURAL AMBASSADORS

The traders have been known as the cultural ambassadors in the past. It is because they facilitated trade, dissemination of ideas, and cultural exchange. They have invented many trade routes throughout the world. With this, they have introduced many goods and technology. The introduction of new technology was done along with the spread of Islamic language and culture. They have played a great role as intermediaries who have fostered cross-cultural interactions. They have also provided many contributions to diversifying and enriching cultures worldwide.

ESTABLISHMENT OF TRADE ROUTES

Muslim traders have played a very important role in the establishment of different trade routes throughout the globe. One of their main establishments was the Silk Road extension. This Silk Road is one of the Ancient trade routes. This road connects East and West and helps facilitate trade in the past. These Muslim traders have also facilitated the exchange of culture, art, and ideas. They have introduced many new Islamic architecture and Islamic languages and developed Islamic cultural habits in the people of different regions. In short, they have left a very long-lasting impact on the cultural landscape.

The traders have also contributed much to the security and safety of the Silk Road. They have protected many merchants as well who trade along these routes. They have played an important role in exchanging knowledge, including medicine, mathematics, and astronomy. Several medicinal and mathematical concepts introduced by Muslim scholars and traders are now used in different parts of the world.

Another important role the Muslim traders have played is in the Trans-Saharan Route. This network of different routes connects North Africa with sub-Saharan Africa. The Muslim traders have been very active in facilitating the trade routes that cross the Sahara desert. They have also established this network for transporting and trading goods through the deserts. They provide facilitation in the exchange of numerous commodities. These commodities include textiles, spices, gold, salt, and ivory. This is because all these commodities were in much demand in the north and sub-Saharan African regions.

So, the Muslim traders served as intermediates in facilitating trade between these two places. The trans-Saharan trade was a good opportunity for the exchange of goods. But along with it was also a good cultural exchange. This is because the Muslim traders have introduced the Arabic language, Muslim religion, and culture to the people in Sub-Saharan Africa. This preaching and cultural exchange greatly impacted the region's language, culture, and religious practices.

KNOWLEDGE DISSEMINATION

The traders have played a very vital role in the dissemination of knowledge in different historical periods. They have been involved in the transmission of scientific as well as mathematics knowledge. It has also influenced culture because Muslim traders have travelled to distant regions to spread architectural knowledge and advanced construction techniques, leading to architectural innovation.

Muslim traders and intellectuals were involved in translating scientific and philosophical works. They provided many translation efforts in different historical periods. They were involved in translating various languages, including Indian, Persian, Roman, and Greek, into Arabic language. All the translations include work from astronomy, medicine, mathematics, natural science, and philosophy. They helped preserve the knowledge of ancient civilisations.

The Muslim traders also played an important role in the House of Wisdom during the Islamic golden age. There was an intellectual centre in Baghdad called Bait ul Hikma, House of Wisdom. It was established in the 9th century till the 13th century. This house of wisdom was mainly dedicated to different translation efforts, advancement, and preservation of knowledge. They also have access to different foreign manuscripts and books. They have also promoted the Arabic language as the main language for trade.

CULTURAL ARTIFACTS AND GOODS

Muslim traders have played a significant role in the exchange of cultural artefacts and goods in history. They have made many contributions in this regard. One of their most important roles was the historic spice trade by establishing different spice roots. They have been instrumental in increasing the global economy for many years. The Muslim traders had direct access to spice-producing regions. These regions include the Middle East, India, and South East Asia. They cultivated different spices and were involved in spice distribution and production.

They have also introduced many new spices that we are using nowadays. These spices include black pepper, cardamom, and ginger, greatly influencing European cuisine. Along with introducing the spices they produced, they have disseminated the culinary knowledge related to spices to the people in the past. The Muslim traders have told important benefits of different spices that have led to the development of traditional medicine and culinary traditions in different areas.

The Muslim traders have also been involved in the trade of textiles and carpets. They were responsible for textile distribution in different areas. These textiles include silk, cotton, and wool, allowing for the textile exchange specific to different cultures. The Muslim traders have also introduced many luxurious textiles into the market. For example, they have introduced silk in the Middle East and European markets.

They have imported it from China and India. It has influenced many new fashion trends and has created a big demand for these luxurious fabrics. Considering the trade of carpets, it was one of the valuable commodities. The hand-woven rugs were the most trending in areas like Persia, Turkey, and Central Asia. So, the textile and carpet trade were also great cultural exchanges in the Islamic world and different regions.

EMBRACE DIVERSITY

The best example of embracing diversity by Muslim traders was the Silk Road. In ancient times, these traders were important in trade facilitation, connecting East and West. They traded many goods with people of different religions and cultures. These people may include Christians, Hindus, or Buddhists. The exchange of goods enriched the diversity of cultures between the people of different regions.

Embracing diversity in trade will promote the idea of International commerce conduction. It will help in recognising the diversity of different products and markets. It involves exploding a new market with consumer preferences. This approach will lead to the expansion of business opportunities and will also increase your revenue. Finding the trading partners and markets will help you mitigate risks associated with the economic downfall or changes in the market demand.

This will also help you stimulate innovation by adapting to different market conditions. The customer preferences will increase the businesses' ability to develop creative products and solutions. It also helps foster goodwill and positive attitudes towards different relationships, leading to better business revenue and outcomes.

ENCOURAGE INTERCULTURAL DIALOGUES

One of the best examples includes the Muslim traders who encouraged the intercultural dialogue in Timbuktu in West Africa. The Muslim traders and scholars made Timbuktu a centre of commerce and learning. The traders from around the world, including North Africa, the Middle East, and the Mediterranean, combined in Timbuktu to encourage trade. They engage in the sharing of goods and ideas, culture, and religious beliefs. This exchange of goods, ideas, language, and beliefs helps them strengthen intercultural dialogues. It resulted in the mixing of African culture into Islamic culture and the progress of both cultures.

One can easily encourage intercultural dialogues through various cultural workshops and events. This is one of the most powerful and innovative ways to promote understanding, appreciation, and respect among diverse communities. Different cultural events show different traditions, cuisines, arts, and history of different ethnicities to hold a workshop educating participants about various traditions and customs. They also encourage those participants to share their own experience and their personal life stories in an open dialogue. These events must be conducted to provide a hands-on cultural experience to different people. All these activities will allow the people to engage in different cultures by collaborating with the local cultural organisations.

The schools and different community groups will be able to host the events and workshops, which will help you bring the diverse chain of participants. It will also be a very innovative way of providing the individuals with a learning opportunity for understanding different cultures of cultural competency training sessions. The sessions will help guide the people from diverse backgrounds. So consider both virtual and in-person events and get a wide audience. This will help you make the intercultural dialogue easily understandable to everyone.

PROMOTE CULTURAL EXCHANGE AS A DRIVER OF ECONOMIC GROWTH

The most common example of promoting cultural exchange by the Muslim traders in the past was the city of Baghdad. It was the best centre where traders from different parts of the world converged and facilitated the exchange of goods and culture. The merchants brought many products from different areas, including Europe, India, China, and Central Asia, to the Baghdad market. The main feature of this trade was the exchange of knowledge and commodities. So many scholars were gathered in Baghdad because of its intellectual and cultural presence.

Promoting cultural exchange for economic growth and standing will benefit the individual and the community. It will increase internal cooperation and harmony. This will also help facilitate cross-cultural learning, including cultural awareness programs and language training. Today, big organisations should increase the partnership between businesses and cultural organisations to promote cultural exchange.

Through collaborative efforts, there will be more success in cross-cultural exchange. One should also promote cultural diplomacy, which will strengthen international relations. It will also help showcase the cultures to diverse festivals, exhibitions, and performances and encourage different government and Nongovernmental organisations to provide cultural awareness. This will help in effective cross-cultural interaction for both diplomatic purposes and for different businesses.

Modern businesses should also support intercultural exchange programs for professionals and artists in different countries. These programs will help in posting the understanding and economic opportunities for the individual. Try to develop and promote different online resources for cross-cultural learning. These may include virtual cultural exchanges, language courses, or other information websites. This will help in providing a great insight into different cultures.

Through all these measures, we can easily strengthen the economic understanding and promote a prosperous and peaceful global community.

INVEST IN EDUCATION AND TRANSLATION

One notable example of Muslim traders investing in education and translation in the past was the Toledo School of Translators. This school was situated in Spain and under Islamic rule for centuries. It was one of the notable translation movements invented by Muslim scholars in the past. Along with the Muslim scholars, the Christian and US scholars collaborated in the translation works. This work includes the translation of Greek and Roman language into the Arabic language. This translation movement helps them in transmitting knowledge to different parts of Europe.

Integration for the employees and promoting the translation of vital documents is a very important step to enhance communication. It will also help remove the language barriers in a workplace comprising diverse cultures. So, the companies should provide training programs or language courses to the Employees. The employees should be given complete access to all the language learning resources. These sources may include online tools, books, magazines, or other applications. One should create a supportive environment for the employees where they can easily learn different types of languages. It would be best if you encouraged language exchange programs for the practice of employees.

The translation of important documents is also very necessary for the employees. Tou should hire highly professional translators to ensure high-quality translations—modern businesses should develop accurate and clear guidelines for professional translators. The guidelines may include terminology consistency, style, preferences, and deadlines. The translations should buy experts and professionals to ensure accuracy. The employees should also be trained in the use of translated documents.

 The translation of the important documents required in your business is very necessary. It should be updated and relevant as your business evolves. Investing in language training and promoting translation can easily reduce communication barriers and create an effective work environment for all employees.

ESTABLISH CULTURAL COMPETENCY TRAINING

Establishing different cultural competency programs is very beneficial for promoting diversity within different organisations. Modern businesses should conduct an assessment to identify specific cultural competency needs and preferences within the organisation. It mainly includes focus groups, interviews, and services. One should outline the main goals and objectives of the cultural competency training programs. Then, create training materials covering all the related cultural competency staff. It may include communication skills, cultural sensitivity, and cultural awareness. It would be best to address communication by fostering an inclusive culture that respects diversity, which is crucial for creating a very equitable and positive workplace.

Generally, top businesses should ensure their leadership is committed to inclusion and diversity. They should also communicate the values and missions of the tasks provided to employees. Moreover, all these principles should be effectively communicated to the employees. This practice ensures that the benefits and compensation provided to employees are fair for all. Therefore, creating an inclusive company culture requires continuous education, determination, and commitment. It helps employees develop more innovative procedures and fosters more productive organisations.

Muslim traders have played the role of intermediaries and cultural ambassadors. They have fostered cultural exchange, cooperation and understanding between the people of diverse regions. All their contribution has played a very important role in shaping the intellectual and cultural landscape of different regions.

Chapter 7

FINANCIAL INSTITUTIONS

The golden age of Islamic civilisation was a period of remarkable advancement in different fields, including culture, economics, science, and medicine. In this vibrant era, Islamic banking and financial systems emerged as the central hub of economic growth and stability. The ancient people followed many unique principles and practices for facilitating commerce through the Silk Road. This also laid the foundation for modern financial Institutions. So, understanding different historical contexts and principles of Islamic Finance in the golden age is essential to learn its significance in the contemporary world.

In the modern world, the global economies face many complex challenges. So, the principles of Islamic finance give a new perspective and innovative solutions for modern businesses. Different concepts, including ethical investment, risk sharing, and interest avoidance, make your business responsible. Moreover, Islamic finance resilience during the economic crisis has increased the importance of International Financial institutions by emphasising their importance in the 21st century.

ISLAMIC BANKING AND FINANCIAL SYSTEMS

Islamic finance is rooted in principles driven by Sharia or Islamic law and emphasises ethical and moral considerations. Islamic finance highly prohibits the payment or acceptance of interest. It also encourages risk sharing between different parties. Financing should also be done by tangible assets or services. It ensures that money is used for protective purposes according to Islamic law. There should be complete transparency in the contracts, avoiding uncertainty or ambiguity. Investment should also adhere to moral and ethical guidelines. According to Islamic law, Islamic finance also encourages the concept of zakat, which helps promote social welfare and wealth distribution.

One of the most prominent real-life examples is the Hawala System, which originated in the Islamic world centuries ago. It is an informal transfer of money which is based on trust. It operates without formal contracts and is widely used in different regions today. The Hawala system shows the principle of transparency, risk sharing and trust in Islamic Finance.

The establishment of the first Islamic Bank by Mit Ghamr Savings Bank in Egypt was also a main example of Islamic Finance. This Bank shows the beginning of the contemporary Islamic banking industry with banks that adhere to the Sharia principles. It also offers a range of financial services, from saving accounts to investment products. This innovation helps lay the foundation for the growth of Islamic financial institutions worldwide.

The establishment of the first Islamic Bank by Mit Ghamr Savings Bank in Egypt was also a main example of Islamic Finance. This Bank shows the beginning of the contemporary Islamic banking industry with banks that adhere to the Sharia principles. It also offers a range of financial services, from saving accounts to investment products. This innovation helps lay the foundation for the growth of Islamic Financial institutions worldwide.

LESSONS FOR MODERN BUSINESSES:

In a world where financial ethics and sustainability are gaining more importance, modern businesses can draw valuable lessons from Islamic finance. Different principles include ethical considerations, transparency, and fairness, which can be integral to financial practices. Modern businesses can easily benefit by adopting ethical finance strategies that are relevant values.

Moreover, the concept of profit-sharing arrangements can also inspire innovation in modern banking. The banks can easily create a more equitable relationship with the customers by avoiding the interest-based models. The profit sharing helps the banks invest in projects with genuine economic value.

ETHICAL INVESTMENT AND SOCIAL RESPONSIBILITY:

Islamic finance places a very strong emphasis on ethical investment as outlined by Sharia, the Islamic legal framework. Various key specifications illustrate that Islamic finance prioritises ethical investment.

From the golden age, Islamic finance prohibits investment in activities that are forbidden or considered haram according to Islamic principles. It includes gambling, alcohol, or interest-based financial activities by avoiding such activities. It ensures that investments are ethically sound and do not contribute to harmful acts.

In the golden age, Islamic finance principles have always promoted risk sharing and fairness in financial transactions. It has encouraged individuals to contribute some of their wealth for charitable purposes. This promotes social responsibility and wealth distribution.

REAL-LIFE EXAMPLES:

Different microfinance initiatives are based on Islamic financial principles, which have integrated Islamic finance to provide financial services to understand and marginalise the community. These initiatives operate on ethical principles by emphasising fairness and profit and loss sharing between the two parties. One notable example is the Akhuwat Foundation. It was founded in 2001 in Pakistan and operates on Karz Al Hasan principles. It provides interest-free loans to empower individuals with low income and entrepreneurs.

PROFIT SHARING AND RISK MITIGATION

Islamic finance mainly depends on profit-sharing and risk-sharing mechanisms. It ensures equitable and ethical transactions in finance. Mudarabah is a partnership contract. In this contract, one party provides the investor, and the other offers expertise and labour. So, the profits are shared according to the pre-agreed ratio. But the losses are borne by investors. This structure helps in encouraging efficient and ethical investment.

While Musharakah has joined a partnership venture, the partners contribute expertise and investment. The profits and losses are shared proportionally based on each partner's contribution. It helps promote risk sharing and investing for the success of the business.

In summary, the golden age of Islamic civilisation introduced key principles of Islamic finance, including interest prohibition and ethical investment, offering valuable lessons for modern businesses seeking responsible and equitable financial practices. Initiatives like the Akhuwat Foundation exemplify the impact of ethical finance on marginalised communities, while partnership contracts like Mudarabah and Musharakah promote ethical investment and risk-sharing. In today's complex economic landscape, the enduring relevance of Islamic finance highlights its potential to shape a more ethical and sustainable financial world.

Chapter **8**

DIPLOMACY AND TREATIES

The era of the Islamic Golden Age became characterised by notable highbrow, cultural, and monetary growth, and at its heart lay the art of trade, international relations, and the crafting of worldwide diplomacy and treaties. These two aspects are the roots of establishing political and trading relationships. Muslim traders and explorers of that time excelled in them with their marvellous negotiation skills and sharp wit.

In this chapter, we will delve into the elaborate interaction among international relations and change through this golden age, discover real-life examples of international relations in movement, and extract treasured instructions that modern agencies can seamlessly combine into their worldwide techniques for fulfilment.

ESTABLISHING TRUST THROUGH CULTURAL EXCHANGES

Trade and international relations throughout this period placed remarkable importance on cultural exchanges. Muslim traders engaged in talk with their overseas counterparts, transcending linguistic and cultural limitations to foster information and trust. These cultural exchanges have been no longer simply superficial gestures; they have been the inspiration upon which diplomatic relationships have been built. By immersing themselves in the customs and traditions of their buying and selling companions, Muslim buyers cultivated an ecosystem of mutual respect and cooperation.

NEGOTIATING FAVORABLE TRADE TERMS

Diplomatic negotiations were the linchpin to securing tremendous exchange terms. These negotiations were a delicate dance, mixing diplomacy and commerce to create useful agreements simultaneously.

The negotiations throughout the Islamic Golden Age were far from one-sided. Muslim buyers had been professional diplomats who understood the art of compromise. They recognised that striking a fair deal became no longer the most beneficial in the short time but crucial for the lengthy-term sustainability of alternate relationships.

To comprehend the importance of alternate international relations during the Islamic Golden Age, let's dive into compelling examples:

Ibn Battuta, the legendary tourist, became not simply a merchant but also a diplomat all through his enormous journeys. His wonderful capacity to navigate numerous cultures and negotiate correctly demonstrated the electricity of international relations in trade. His travels took him via many regions and civilisations, together with the lands of Islam, Africa, Europe, and Asia. In each area, he failed to conduct commercial enterprise and engaged in international relations.

Apart from that, the Silk Road, a sprawling network of exchange routes, epitomised the fusion of cultures and commerce. It was through diplomacy that this historic trade artery remained open and prosperous for centuries. It was more than an alternate course; it became the assembly point of civilisations. It connected the East and West, enabling the exchange of items, thoughts, cultures, and technology.

LESSONS FOR MODERN BUSINESS

Recognise the role of trade diplomacy in building trust and cooperation

Diplomacy extends far beyond the ink on a treaty. It's approximately nurturing relationships based on acceptance as true with and cooperation, cornerstones of sustained achievement in the global alternate. In the cutting-edge commercial enterprise global, trust is a forex greater value than any. Trust is the idea upon which change-making relationships are built and sustained.

INVEST IN CULTURAL UNDERSTANDING AS A FOUNDATION FOR SUCCESSFUL INTERNATIONAL TRADE.

In today's worldwide market, cultural sensitivity may be an amazing asset. Understanding and respecting the cultures of your trade companions can be important for fruitful collaborations. International commercial enterprise is now not limited to borders; it transcends cultures and languages. By investing in cultural understanding, groups can bridge the gap among unique worlds.

THE IMPORTANCE OF TREATIES WITHIN THE ISLAMIC GOLDEN AGE

Treaties served as the bedrock of peaceful trade among family members during the Islamic Golden Age. Two exemplary treaties come to the fore—the Treaty of Hudaybiyyah and the Treaty of Najran—with Christian groups.

The Treaty of Hudaybiyyah signed between the Prophet Muhammad and the Quraysh tribe, is a first-rate instance of diplomatic acumen. Though the terms were regarded as adverse to the Muslims at the time, the treaty, in the long run, caused a prolonged period of peace. This demonstrates the significance of searching beyond immediate profits and thinking about the lengthy-term benefits of diplomatic agreements.

The Treaty of Najran with Christian Communities epitomised the inclusivity of Islamic diplomacy, bearing in mind harmonious coexistence and flourishing trade with Christian communities. This treaty exemplifies the spirit of inclusivity in Islamic diplomacy. It granted Christian groups the liberty to practice their religion and engage in trade without fear of persecution. This commitment to religious freedom created a climate of tolerance and cooperation conducive to alternate.

In 1494, the Treaty of Tordesillas divided newly observed lands past Europe between Portugal and Spain. This historic agreement underscores the importance of formal treaties in shaping international relations.

The Treaty of Nanking in 1842 marked China's reluctant beginning of foreign exchange, showcasing how treaties would be instrumental in gaining access to new markets.

LESSONS FOR MODERN BUSINESS

Understand the Value of Formal Agreements in International Trade

Formal treaties and agreements offer a framework for alternates, supplying felony protections and clarity that benefit all events involved. In the contemporary complex worldwide alternate landscape, formal agreements are not the most effective, useful, or crucial. They offer a solid criminal foundation that protects the interests of all parties involved. Modern organisations have to prioritise the drafting and adherence to such agreements to ensure the smooth operation of worldwide trade.

ENSURE TREATY COMPLIANCE TO MAINTAIN TRUST AND LONG-TERM PARTNERSHIPS.

Compliance with treaty obligations is pivotal for nurturing belief and fostering enduring partnerships in international exchange. Trust is the lifeblood of international business. Compliance with treaty duties demonstrates a dedication to the agreements made, and it serves as a cornerstone of acceptance as true in worldwide alternate relationships. Businesses honouring their commitments are more likely to construct robust, long-term partnerships with their international counterparts.

THE INTERCONNECTEDNESS OF DIPLOMACY AND TRADE IN THE ISLAMIC GOLDEN AGE

During the Islamic Golden Age, international relations and exchange were intricately intertwined. Diplomatic missions served as enablers of trade and gateways to new markets.

DIPLOMATIC MISSIONS AS TRADE ENABLERS

Ambassadors and diplomats played pivotal roles in beginning new trade routes and markets. They acted as cultural bridges, facilitating interactions between diverse civilisations. In the Islamic Golden Age, diplomatic missions were not just about replacing pleasantries; they were instrumental in expanding trade networks. Ambassadors and diplomats served as conduits for trade, assisting merchants in navigating overseas territories and setting up connections that caused rich exchange.

LEVERAGING DIPLOMACY FOR MARKET ACCESS

The diplomats of the Islamic Golden Age understood that diplomacy became a way to stop and that cease became regularly advanced to get entry to profitable markets. Through skilful negotiations and diplomatic finesse, they opened doorways to new trade opportunities.

THE ROLE OF EMBASSIES AND CONSULATES IN MODERN TRADE RELATIONS

Embassies and consulates function as pivotal hubs for promoting alternate hobbies and resolving change-related disputes, showcasing the enduring relevance of diplomacy in international commerce.

Modern embassies and consulates are not simply bureaucratic offices but lively proponents of exchange. They guide groups by navigating complicated regulatory landscapes, supporting trade-associated problems, and fostering connections among local and foreign partners.

Bilateral and Multilateral Trade Agreements of the Twenty-First Century

Bilateral and multilateral change agreements are the epitome of diplomatic collaboration in the current generation. They function as frameworks for international alternatives, streamlining strategies, decreasing change barriers, and promoting financial growth on an international scale. These agreements spotlight the symbiotic relationship between diplomacy and alternatives.

LESSONS FOR MODERN BUSINESS

Modern companies need to wholeheartedly include diplomacy as a tool for dismantling trade limitations and advocating for exchange-friendly policies.

DIPLOMACY IS A TOOL FOR BREAKING DOWN TRADE BARRIERS.

The present-day business panorama faces regulatory challenges, from customs processes to highbrow belongings rights. Diplomacy allows us to engage with governments and regulate our bodies to address these challenges. By working intently with diplomatic missions and authority companies, businesses can recommend adjustments that allow smoother operational changes.

USE DIPLOMATIC CHANNELS TO ADVOCATE FOR TRADE-FRIENDLY POLICIES.

Engaging actively with diplomatic missions and participating in exchange-associated discussions empowers businesses to persuade coverage selections that once affect their operations.

BUILDING STRONG DIPLOMATIC TIES

Islamic diplomats employed an array of strategies, such as cultural change packages and hosting foreign envoys, to beef up diplomatic ties.

CULTURAL EXCHANGE PROGRAMMES

At some point in the Islamic Golden Age, cultural alternate programmes have now been more than mere gestures of goodwill; they have been strategic investments in diplomacy. By sharing their cultures, know-how, and traditions, diplomats constructed bridges of expertise that transcended borders and paved the way for fruitful diplomatic relationships.

HOSTING FOREIGN ENVOYS

Hosting overseas envoys became more than just a show of courtesy; it became a diplomatic method. It created an ecosystem of appreciation and consideration conducive to successful negotiations. By treating overseas guests with honour and generosity, diplomats ensured that the observed negotiations were performed in a high-quality and cooperative spirit.

THE ROLE OF CULTURAL DIPLOMACY IN MODERN INTERNATIONAL RELATIONS

Cultural diplomacy is crucial for nations to promote their values and interests globally, cultivating goodwill and favourable perceptions. It goes beyond formal negotiations, creating an environment of cooperation and change.

Businesses frequently engage in diplomatic endeavours to cultivate relationships with overseas companions, regulators, and stakeholders. This underscores the strategic significance of international relations in worldwide commerce.

LESSONS FOR MODERN BUSINESS

To enhance their worldwide exchange endeavours, modern-day companies ought to invest in building long-term relationships with foreign partners and embody cultural sensitivity.

INVEST IN BUILDING LONG-TERM RELATIONSHIPS WITH FOREIGN PARTNERS

Strong and enduring relationships are frequently the bedrock of successful worldwide exchange ventures. Modern businesses should adopt an angle that extends past quick-time profits. Just as Islamic diplomats invest in long-term relationships, agencies must prioritise cultivating lasting partnerships with their global opposites. These partnerships can overcome challenges and create possibilities for sustained growth.

CULTURAL SENSITIVITY CAN BE A POWERFUL ASSET IN INTERNATIONAL TRADE

Understanding and respecting the cultural nuances of foreign markets can result in smoother negotiations and more fruitful partnerships. In a globalised world, cultural sensitivity isn't just a matter of courtesy but a strategic advantage. Businesses that take time to apprehend and respect the cultural intricacies of their buying and selling companions are better positioned to build trust, navigate complexities, and capture possibilities that would elude folks who brush aside those essential issues.

Overall, the Islamic Golden Age is a testament to the enduring relevance of international relations and treaties within commerce. By embracing these classes, modern businesses can write their personal fulfilment memories and contribute to the ongoing legacy of international relations worldwide. As they forge new connections and break down obstacles, they pave the way for a future where international relations continue to be the bridge that spans the various international aspects of worldwide commerce.

CONCLUSION

As we conclude, Muslims from the Islamic Golden Age, whether diplomats or shipbuilders, traders or intellectuals, have left behind a valuable roadmap for the modern world. The House of Wisdom in Baghdad, along with other centres of intellectual activity, fostered knowledge exchange among scholars from diverse backgrounds, teaching us the importance of emphasising the value of diversity and global cooperation. The development of navigational instruments like the astrolabe and quadrant by scholars like Al-Fazari and Al-Zarqali revolutionised sea travel. It contributed to safer exploration, offering a lesson in the innovation of traditional methods. Moreover, we can learn about engineering advancements from the elegant design and versatility of dhows crafted by skilled Arab shipbuilders.

While the contemporary Muslim world faces economic challenges, the overall history of the Islamic Golden Age provides insights into the rich history of Muslim exploration, trade, and intellectual pursuits. Therefore, Muslims' success in diverse fields can teach modern businesses to establish strong diplomatic relationships, explore new business routes, invest in intellectual activities, and grow their businesses through trade hubs.

FINAL SUMMARY

The Golden Islamic Age was a remarkable period between the 8th and 13th centuries that gave way to several practices being used in today's modern era. Despite the stereotypical norms, Muslims were popular and very influential. In fact, they were the ones who introduced the creation of paper using a Chinese process, which Europe later adopted. With the newfound ability to keep better records, they significantly impacted developing civilisations and the sharing of knowledge.

As renowned travellers of the Islamic Golden Age, they introduced Dhow ships and later established trade routes through Northern Africa, Spain, Andalusia, and Central Asia, with the Silk Road being the most popular. With a wealth of knowledge to share with the world, they were one of the first eras to introduce copywriting. Whether they were shipbuilders, traders or otherwise, the roadmap they left has and will continue to impact the modern age as we know it significantly.

www.ingramcontent.com/pod-product-compliance
Lightning Source LLC
Chambersburg PA
CBHW080852120626
46546CB00008B/2792